T0315935

IMMORTALITY

IMMORTALITY

THE CHRISTIAN VIEW

A Lecture to Churchmen
at Norwich
11 FEB. 1931
by
ALEXANDER NAIRNE, D.D.

CAMBRIDGE
AT THE UNIVERSITY PRESS
1931

CAMBRIDGE
UNIVERSITY PRESS

University Printing House, Cambridge CB2 8BS, United Kingdom

Published in the United States of America by Cambridge University Press, New York

Cambridge University Press is part of the University of Cambridge.

It furthers the University's mission by disseminating knowledge in the pursuit of education, learning and research at the highest international levels of excellence.

www.cambridge.org
Information on this title: www.cambridge.org/9781107638846

© Cambridge University Press 1931

First published 1931
Re-issued 2014

A catalogue record for this publication is available from the British Library

ISBN 978-1-107-63884-6 Paperback

IMMORTALITY: THE CHRISTIAN VIEW

A great theme is here proposed. Hope, desire, the age-long common sense of mankind, the dignity as well as the imbecility of our mortality and vocation, are to be considered. But there is no place for fancy. It is the Christian view that we are to elucidate, and the Christian view includes the life on earth, the heroic death, and the resurrection of Him whom the Christian calls Lord and Saviour.

The Christian view of immortality is first of all the moral view. And that does not imply reward and punishment in a future life beyond the grave, except so far as reasonable assurance of such reward and punishment induces Christ-likeness here and now. And Christian immortality is quality not extension, the immediate enjoyment of the eternal "while it is called to-day". That is possible for others besides those who name Jesus Christ as Lord. But it is easier for such as do, for the Christian trusts the Father with the trust wherewith the Lord Jesus trusted. "God is the God of the living : all live unto him" begins and consummates the Christian view.

Let me begin by quoting a notable confession of faith in immortality :—

No coward soul is mine,
No trembler in the world's storm-troubled sphere:
I see heaven's glories shine,
And faith shines equal, arming me from fear.

O God within my breast,
Almighty, ever present Deity !
Life—that in me has rest,
As I—undying Life—have power in Thee !

Vain are the thousand creeds
That move men's hearts; unalterably vain;
Worthless as withered weeds,
Or idlest froth amid the boundless main,

To waken doubt in one
Holding so fast by thine infinity;
So surely anchor'd on
The steadfast rock of immortality.

With wide-embracing love
Thy Spirit animates eternal years,
Pervades and broods above,
Changes, sustains, dissolves, creates and rears.

Though earth and man were gone
And suns and universes cease to be,
And Thou wert left alone,
Every existence would exist in Thee.

There is not room for Death,
Nor atom that his might could render void:
Thou—Thou art Being and Breath,
And what Thou art may never be destroyed.

Those are Emily Brontë's "Last Lines". They
have been called Stoic, but are Christian. Chris-
tians may add, some this some that, but may not
abstract from this full flood of faith, and what
they add of detail must be reverent and restrained,

self-mortifying: If any would save his soul...he must lose it, for the Saviour's sake and his good-tidings.

Benjamin Jowett, the famous Master of Balliol, is honest faithful and assuring in his Introduction to Plato's *Phaedo*:

Most persons when the last hour comes are re-signed to the order of nature and the will of God.... Another life must be described, if at all, in forms of thought and not of sense.... We cannot reason from the natural to the spiritual, or from the outward to the inward.... Most people have been content to rest their belief in immortality on the agreement of the more enlightened part of mankind, and on the in-separable connexion of such a doctrine with the existence of a God...also on the impossibility of doubting about the continued existence of those whom we love and reverence in this world. And after all has been said, the figure, the analogy, the argument, are felt to be only approximations in different forms of the common sentiment of the human heart.

One silence there is in Emily Brontë's poem

which Christian faith would fill. Hear Donne,
A Hymn to God the Father:

> Wilt thou forgive that sin where I begun,
> Which was my sin...through which I still
> Do run...though still I do deplore?
>> When thou hast done thou hast not done,
>> For I have more.
>
> Wilt thou forgive that sin which I have won
> Others to sin...?
>> When thou hast done thou hast not done, etc.
>
> I have a sin of fear, that when I have spun
> My last thread, I shall perish on the shore:
> But swear by thyself, that at my death thy Son
> Shall shine as he shines now and heretofore:
>> And having done this thou hast done,
>> I fear no more.

You catch the pious wit of the seventeenth century, the pun on his own name and on Sun and Son. But you catch the deep meaning too. Since the Son of God was born and died and dying lives, man in God, all life is different. Trust is now

(9)

assured, and affects even where it is not con-
fessed. Emily Brontë would not have been so
firm and free and deep but for him whom she
names not, but who has redeemed her and us and
all mankind.

And her almost rejection of creeds should not
offend a churchman; for in comparison with that
boundless main of hers creeds are but froth: and
there are some good churchmen to whom creeds
are less help than hindrance, as to her.

Yet not so, taken rightly. The earliest creeds
were hymns, like that fragment in the Epistle to
Timothy "Who was manifested in the flesh...
received up in glory", or the *Te Deum*. And the
early name for creed was *symbolum*. A creed was
poetry, symbolic, not plain statement of plain
fact. Repeat the Apostles' Creed thoughtfully
and consider the extraordinary character of every
sentence. It is thought, affection, mystery,
sketched and abruptly sketched, in picture: yet
hardly picture; you think of that surprising
definition Plato gives of "form"—"form always

follows colour". The Apostles' Creed in its original is Latin. The Latin "eternal" is better than our English translation "everlasting", but our "body" is truer to the sense than its "flesh". But take the whole without too scrupulous a nicety over details. What free glad simplicity; the faith of the people and the catacombs, whereas the Nicene Creed is theology of doctors and councils, yet that too so grand and satisfying and still so poetic. And then there is "The Hymn *Quicunque vult*" which we call the Athanasian Creed, wherein immortality enforces salutary discipline, a bond of hope for every day:

One Christ...God and Man...One, not by conversion of the Godhead into flesh: but by taking of the Manhood into God...Who suffered for our salvation: descended into hell, rose again the third day from the dead....He ascended into heaven, he sitteth on the right hand of the Father, God Almighty: from whence he shall come to judge the quick and the dead. At whose coming all men shall rise again with their bodies: and shall give account for their own works. And they that have done good shall go

into life everlasting: and they that have done evil
into everlasting fire. This is the Catholic Faith.

How broad and deep, wonderful and homely.
Good deeds and evil are the ultimate matter: He
died to make us good.

Wonderful the mystery of his life and fate and
person: but the same wonder throughout the life
of men: "For as the reasonable soul and flesh is
one man, so God and man is one Christ". The
Word became flesh, the Incarnation: what is it
like? what is it all a piece with? Answer: The
soul and body making every man a person, a
spirit. And so the Resurrection:

How say some among you that there is no resurrection of the dead? But if there is no resurrection
of the dead, neither hath Christ been raised: and if
Christ hath not been raised, then is our preaching
vain and your faith is also vain...for if the dead are
not raised neither hath Christ been raised; and if
Christ hath not been raised your faith is vain, ye are
yet in your sins.

S. Paul is quick to believe that Christ has

risen because he recognises in the rising of Christ the proper sequel of "Christian" history: his faith as Pharisee commends his faith as Apostle; his faith as Apostle assures the faith of the Pharisee: "But now hath Christ been raised from the dead, the firstfruits of them that are asleep".

So Paul to the Corinthians. And the quotation reminds us that creeds are bound to holy Scripture. They are not independent authority: they are but symbols summaries interpretations of Scripture.

Thus the Fire in the Athanasian Creed is not penal but that fire at the end of the Apocalypse of S. John which consumes and abolishes evil finally utterly eternally, leaving the whole world free pure and glad for the coming of Jesus the Lord: "And there shall be no curse any more... and the Spirit and the bride say, Come. And he that is athirst, let him come....Yea: I come quickly. Amen: come, Lord Jesus".

And so each and every sentence in the creeds

about the Advent and the Judgement must be interpreted in the light of S. Paul's

Then cometh the end, when he shall deliver up the kingdom to God, even the Father; when he shall have abolished all rule and all authority and power. For he must reign till he hath put all his enemies under his feet...and when all things have been subjected...then shall the Son also himself be subjected to him that did subject all things unto him, that God may be all in all.

Deep and dark with excess of light. Beyond Judgement the End, beyond time the eternal, beyond evolution the absolute: abstract credal sentences, God the concrete unity. Compare the noble envoi of Dampier Whetham's *History of Science and its relations with Philosophy and Religion*:

But, now or later, intelligible mechanism will fail, and we shall be left face to face with the awful mystery which is reality.

And S. Paul to Corinthians passes into S. Paul to Ephesians with that far-reaching vista of progress and growth to which he corrected his early expectation of an immediate Advent Day: "The building up of the body of Christ till we all attain unto the unity of the faith, unto one full-grown man, unto the measure of the stature of the fulness of Christ". He has passed quite away from the picturesque tradition of the Jewish Church, the Clouds and Trumpet, to the deeper Jewish theology of the representative inclusive Messiah, and developes that along the line of the Christian allegiance to the Lord Jesus. He believes in the Christ who is not just the Lord Jesus of the days of the flesh, but Jesus with all who are his disciples, yea all mankind ultimately whom he redeemed. These are in real being his body. With them he grows into perfection, one Christ not by conversion of Godhead into flesh, but by taking of manhood into God; and the Advent: "Ring in the Christ that is to be".

And still the deep, natural, surprising apostolic faith proceeds. S. Paul lets the picture go, but keeps the plan of time. S. John presently goes even deeper than that—deeper and strangely simpler—penetrating through the veil of time itself to an eternal Now. The Master goes, but going comes; for his going is to the Father, and opens the mansion of the Spirit here and now to his trusting and loving disciples. Eternal life is here and now. Death is less accounted of than the passage in abundant life through the door of charity into the mansion of the Spirit: and the life eternal is to know the Father as the one true God, and Jesus whom the Father sent to die, to live; and judgement is the discerning influence of that Light which lightens history and conscience here and now.

There are two lines in our pattern, two strains of the one truth—for truth (as we get it) is counter-strained like the never resting arch—eternal life here and now: resurrection of the body and judgement to come.

So in Old Testament. The faith of the patriarchs is presented as the trust of pilgrims on earth who are tent-friends of God: "For I am a nomad with thee, a sojourner as all my fathers were". And then: I am here no more but I go hence and am still with God, and that is enough; I ask no more questions; Into thy hands I commend my spirit; I shall be satisfied when I awake with thy likeness.

But questions were asked, and the vulgar fell back on the pagan semitic superstition of Sheol, the Hell, the Pit, the shadowy house of death in life cut off from the care of God. But the prophets would have none of that. More and more clearly they proclaimed one God, the one Lord, all merciful, no place or state beyond his care. "Isaiah is very bold" as you remember; "I am the LORD and there is none beside: I form the light and create darkness: I make peace and create evil. I am the LORD that doeth all these things". These prophets do not say much about a future life beyond the grave, but they believe in the living God and all life as life in him. Then the prophets, failing in their own time, left their faith to grow firm in succeeding generations;

and what was true—for there was a germ of truth—in the doctrines of Sheol was purged and gathered into it. And in Maccabean days of persecution the gallant venture of a more expressive faith was dared, strong heart co-operating with trustful reason, and the resurrection and judgement, triumph of saints and shame of tyrants became an article of the pharisaic creed. Thus it appears at the end of the book of Daniel and in that serene vision of Jeremiah in Maccabees as the old saint still praying for the people. But Sirach protests for the quiet large charitable ancient trust:

O death, how bitter is the remembrance of thee to a
    man that is at peace in his possessions,
Unto a man that hath nothing to distract him and
    hath prosperity in all things,
And that still hath strength to receive meat!
O death, acceptable is thy sentence unto a man that
    is needy and that faileth in strength,
That is in extreme old age, and is distracted about all
    things,
And is perverse and hath lost patience.
Fear not the sentence of death!

Remember them that have been before thee and that
    come after:
This is the sentence from the Lord over all flesh,
And why dost thou refuse when it is the pleasure of
    the Most High?
Whether it be ten or a hundred or a thousand years
There is no inquisition of life in the grave.

S. Hierome decreed that Sirach might be read
for good manners not for doctrine. Yet the conscience of men has been too strong for his authority,
and there is something like this in the Epistle of
S. Peter and even in Romans, and to-day "the
doom of reason writ in man's soul and heart" induces many to wish that Sirach's plain kindly
trust might be allowed within the Christian view
of immortality.

And may it not? Beyond councils and creeds,
beyond S. Paul, the Christian appeal goes back to
the Lord Jesus himself.

Hear him in the Galilean Gospels: "But that
the dead are raised, even Moses shewed, when he
called the Lord the God of Abraham, and the God

of Isaac, and the God of Jacob. Now he is not the God of the dead, but of the living: for all live unto him". And, "Father, into thy hands I commend my spirit", goes back to the breadth and depth and reticence of the Psalter; as did the Ecclesiast: "or ever the silver cord be loosed, or the golden bowl be broken...and the dust return to the earth as it was, and the spirit return unto God who gave it". Thus Psalmist Saviour and Sceptic all rest at last on the promise of Genesis, "the doom of reason written on man's heart and conscience" when man was first elaborated from chaos and the brute world, when conscience and affection began and the Lord God formed man of the dust of the ground and breathed into his nostrils the breath of life and man became a living soul, and God created man in his own image: In the beginning the Word was with God, was God, all things were made by him, in him was life and the life was the light of men, and the Word became flesh and dwelt among us.

There is the one unfathomable ocean of our trust, the Christian view of immortality.

And the Gospel according to S. John is the incomparable interpretation of that sojourn of the Word: Ecce Homo: the story of Galilean intercourse affection trust, discipleship deepening into heart-to-heartedness: of Martha Mary and Lazarus, of the Last Supper and its colloquy and prayer and theology, the many mansions and the progress from the mansion of the senses to the mansion of the Spirit, memory burgeoning into a mode of life eternal, and the going to the Father inaugurates the communion of saints, the union here and now of Master and disciples in the Father, of him and all who trust him and accept his invitation to go with him to the Father and be made sons together just as he is, all within the very Godhead perfected into one, all living, all loving with pure reality of the mansion of the Spirit, aweful yet homely:

As many as received him, to them gave he the right to become children of God:

And the glory which thou hast given me I have given unto them: that they may be one, even as we are one: I in them and thou in me, that they may be perfected into one:

A new commandment I give unto you that ye love one another even as I have loved you:

and

We know that we have passed out of death into life, because we love the brethren.

What certainty of immortality can be added to that? Life in God; that one Man, the Master, our Lord and God; we and our friends so frail and sinful, yet his disciples, with him, within the Godhead. There, in that communion of saints is the true and perfect resurrection and life, here and now, continually renewed as generation passes into generation, active rejoicing sorrowing, passing away, all one, all living in God, already passed out of death into life, *mundo maiore sive communi*: "By this shall all men know that ye are my disciples if ye have love one to another".

(22)

Love *caritas* ἀγάπη: the Christian view, the Christian dogma.

Yet is it so indeed? Would the great universal Church endorse this?

Hear Selden in his *Table Talk*:

> A glorious church is like a magnificent feast; there is all the variety that may be, but every one chooses out a dish or two that he likes and lets the rest alone: how glorious so ever the church is every one chooses out of it his own religion, by which he governs himself, and lets the rest alone.... To know what was believed in all ages the way is to consult the liturgies not any private man's writings. As if you would know how the church of England serves God, go to the Common Prayer Book, consult not this or that man.

Does not the Prayer Book contradict this lecture? The Prayer Book says little of eternal life here and now but much of this world and the world to come; it does proclaim in certain passages of supreme devotion the mystical communion but more often and more obviously the future resurrection, judgement, and the hope of heaven.

Yes, but there is no contradiction herein. A like variety appears in Scripture; even in this very Gospel according to S. John, as in the narrative of the Galilean breakfast in ch. xxi after the philosophic theology of the Last Supper in chs. xiv–xvii; or in close juxtaposition in chs. v and vi—"Marvel not at this: for the hour cometh (in spite of the preceding '…and now is…'), in which all that are in the tombs shall hear his voice, and shall come forth; they that have done good unto the resurrection of life; and they that have done evil unto the resurrection of judgement". This is the Johannine explication of what the Saviour's word in the earlier record implies: "Have ye understood these things? They say unto him, Yea. And he said unto them, Therefore every scribe who hath been made a disciple unto the kingdom of heaven is like unto a man that is a householder, which bringeth forth out of his treasure things new and old". New and old:

the new thoughtful exposition, closer to the sense; the old Hebrew picture-language, stirring simple hearts: no language perfectly adequate to divine mysteries; sincerity and charity make essential understanding. Only the time does come to most minds late or soon when the old childlike beauty must yield to the new manly reflection; and then the words of the Johannine Saviour are ready in the treasury. For such does the Johannine Gospel prove its purpose again and again. The evangelist looks back to Galilean words and works and days; but through a veil of far memory, long intercourse in spirit, hopes, perplexities, ideas of a new generation: and perhaps this evangelist is twyform; one of that new generation wrote out the beloved disciple's oral instructions and composed the whole into the "Gospel according to...", interpreting still as still fresh questions pressed upon the inexhaustible inexpressible truth:

And there are also many other things which Jesus did, the which if they should be written every one,

I suppose that even the world itself would not contain the books that should be written.

So only and perhaps so best we discern "the ancient as if ghostly beauty of outlines". We essay in vain to reduce the rich vitality of the Gospels to a pattern—Schweitzer's Kingdom, Seeley's King, the modern homeliness, Renan's Galilean lustre. Yet colour is there before outline, and this deep colour of large eternity holds all, and now and again gleams forth of this and that incontestably authentic act or word.

"Consult not this or that man." And yet some counsellors are good, and not least some who startle us by unexpected sympathy. No longer "lieth the whole world in the evil" as when the little flock kept the faith in Ephesus. That little flock has permeated the world. The good Shepherd did not give his life in vain. Secular philosophers are confluent with orthodox divinity to-day. Tennyson the poet, F. H. Bradley the metaphysician, join hands with Hort for the interpretation of S. John.

Bradley in his latter days, replying to some whom his causticity in *Appearance and Reality* had offended, wrote in his *Essays on Truth and Reality*:

To die and go we know not where, to survive as ourselves and yet to become we know not what—such thoughts must always bring disquiet. If we are left with that and with no more than that, we have obviously some cause for apprehension. It is here that religion, if we have a decent religion, should come to our aid. Any but an inferior religion must on one hand condemn all self-seeking after death. But on the other hand it will assure us that all evil is really overcome, and that victory (even if we do not understand how) lies with the good.

And in the end the argument that we are finished when our bodies have decayed seems to possess but a small degree of logical evidence. Death may be an overmastering impression, but it is certainly no necessary truth, and the poet was perhaps not wrong when he called it "a mockery".

Finally he adds this latest comment on his own words:

The reference is to Shelley's *Sensitive Plant*. I do

not know whether this in my case is a mark of senility, but I find myself taking more and more as literal fact what I used in my youth to admire and love as poetry.

Here are the concluding stanzas of Shelley's poem:

> Whether that lady's gentle mind,
> No longer with the form combined
> Which scattered love, as stars do light,
> Found sadness, where it left delight,
>
> I dare not guess; but in this life
> Of error, ignorance, and strife,
> Where nothing is, but all things seem,
> And we the shadows of the dream,
>
> It is a modest creed, and yet
> Pleasant if one considers it,
> To own that death itself must be,
> Like all the rest, a mockery.
>
> That garden sweet, that lady fair,
> And all sweet shapes and colours there,
> In truth have never past away:
> 'Tis we, 'tis ours are changed; not they.

For love, and beauty, and delight,
There is no death nor change; their might
Exceeds our organs, which endure
No light, being themselves obscure.

That is Johannine. Mark the series:

S. PAUL: death is the wages of sin: the last enemy.
EPISTLE TO HEBREWS: death is perfecting.
S. JOHN: death is lost in life.

www.ingramcontent.com/pod-product-compliance
Ingram Content Group UK Ltd.
Pitfield, Milton Keynes, MK11 3LW, UK
UKHW042327020325
455765UK00001B/2